Give God Some Credit

Risk Taking
for Greater Impact

Brett Andrews

Give God Some Credit: Risk Taking for Greater Impact

Copyright © 2015 by Brett Andrews
ISBN: 978-0-9887411-2-6

Exponential is a growing movement of leaders committed to the spread of healthy new churches. Exponential Resources spotlights and spreads actionable principles, ideas and solutions for the accelerated multiplication of healthy, reproducing faith communities. For more information, visit exponential.org

All rights reserved. No part of this book – including the icons and images - may be reproduced in any manner whatsoever without prior written permission from copyright holder, except where noted in the text and in the case of brief quotations embodied in critical articles and reviews.

This book is manufactured in the United States.

Unless otherwise indicated, all Scripture quotations are taken from the Holy Bible, New International Version, copyright © 1973, 1978, 1984, 2011 by International Bible Society. All emphases in Scripture quotations have been added by the author.

Edited by Lindy Lowry
Cover Design and Layout by E Reiss and Story.GS

Acknowledgements

I want to thank the crew at Passion for Planting for sponsoring this book. No group has served church planters the way that Dale Spaulding and Pat Furgerson have through the years. Every year thousands of churches get a healthier start because of their free resources. Please check out the Passion for Planting website at http://church-planting.net.

A special thanks to the crew at Exponential. Eric Reiss, Lindy Lowry, and Karen Pheasant are worthy of all the praise they receive.

I am also deeply indebted to the staff and leadership team of New Life Christian Church with whom I have been privileged to serve for over two decades. Specifically, to the Ron Furgerson clan: You have been my family and ministry partners for nearly thirty years. Great is your reward in heaven!

Creed Branson, some people serve in the background in a way that still garners attention and credit to themselves. Your competence makes the rest of us shine, while you draw no praise for yourself in the background. You are rare. Great is your reward in heaven!

Finally, to my long-suffering and wise companion, Laura. No one has sacrificed more to let God build His church at New Life than you.

Inside

Introduction

**Chapter 1
If You Can Dream**

**Chapter 2
Multiplication Tensions**

**Chapter 3
We Messed Up, So You Don't Have To**

About the Author

Introduction

He came at me with fire in his eyes. Good-humored fire, but fire nonetheless.

"Why didn't you ever tell me?" he said.

"Why didn't I tell you what?"

"I was on staff with you for two years," he said. "You never told me about your frustration! All these years, I thought I was the only one who felt frustrated!"

Fresh out of his internship in Louisville, Kentucky, Vince joined our staff to become our first church planter. After two years, we sent him out to plant a new work in Virginia Beach. (Yes, God sends some to Nineveh and some to Bangladesh; Vince got the beach.)

Recently, Vince read one of my sermons in which I shared a secret: For the first thirteen years of paid ministry, I felt like quitting every year. At some point, I would wind up saying to myself, *I can't do this. The task, the need, and the demands far exceed what I have to offer. The calling is big. I am small.*

Since sharing my feelings of inadequacy, I've been surprised by the number of ministers who have told me they've had the same feelings, the same shared experience. Many of them believe that the minister is *never* equal to the message and that the one called is *never* equal to the call. In fact, anytime a minister feels equal to his/her ministry, I would question his/her grasp on reality. The pastor who can go to bed at night feeling perfectly adequate either suffers from a myopic kingdom vision or an exaggerated sense of self.

I remember reading about how Abraham Lincoln once looked at himself and the American people and concluded, "God must love common people. He made so many of them." I love that.

I also love that the apostle Paul said that God is "able to do far more abundantly than all that we ask or think, according to the power at work within us " (Eph. 3:20). Individually, these references from Lincoln and Paul are two wonderful feel-good platitudes. Combine them, and you have something pretty powerful. God calls common people to accomplish far beyond their ability to imagine. For His glory. By His power. This book is written for common people who carry the burden for increased impact.

If you're looking for a book about an impressive church with exceptional leaders and their dramatic stories, do a Google search. You'll discover no shortage of those books. But that's not what you'll find here. This is the story of New Life Christian Church in the northern Virginia suburbs of Washington D.C. Our ambitions have always exceeded our abilities. Our desire has always been to be a high-impact, regularly reproducing, church-planting church.

In the spirit of Peter's letters to the churches, I doubt you'll discover anything "new" in the following pages, but I pray that as you read our story you'll be stirred to some righteous thinking. Perhaps, your vision will be stretched. Perhaps, you'll pick up a few pointers from our experience. Perhaps, not. Above all, I hope you'll find encouragement to climb higher. If God can do anything through our church, He can do great things through yours. In the words of the great missionary William Carey, "expect great things of God; attempt great things for God."

It's time.

Chapter 1
If You Can Dream

If church planting means learning to live in the tension, then every church planter should read English poet Rudyard Kipling's poem, *If*, at least once a year. It begins:

> *If you can keep your head when all about you*
> *Are losing theirs and blaming it on you,*
> *If you can trust yourself when all men doubt you,*
> *But make allowance for their doubting too;*
> *If you can wait and not be tired by waiting,*
> *Or being lied about, don't deal in lies,*
> *Or being hated, don't give way to hating,*
> *And yet don't look too good, nor talk too wise:*
> *If you can dream—and not make dreams your master;*

Every church planter dreams. Ask any planter before opening day what he/she dreams the church will look like in five years, and he/she will paint you a brilliant portrait. But dreams aren't always advantageous. They can lead a church planter into, or away from, Jerusalem. Godly dreams pursued in godly ways with godly motives in God's power lead us to experience immeasurably more than we could ask or imagine. However, dreams that appear godly and are pursued with mixed motives in the power of clever strategies lead to frustration, or even more tragically, to the flourishing of our flesh. Dreams are not neutral. They are either God's servants, or, like Kipling observed, they become our masters.

The New Life Christian story is about people who have struggled to dream—and not make dreams their master.

The Birth of a Dream
"You gotta see the baby! You gotta see the baby!"

Every *Seinfeld* fan knows the mantra that runs throughout "The Hamptons" episode (or better known as the "ugly baby" episode). Jerry, Elaine, George and Kramer travel to the Hamptons to see their friends' newborn. Then, they see the baby. As the father dotes and the mother drones on, "Isn't he gorgeous," Jerry and Elaine turn their heads away. Later, Elaine shares her true emotions with another guest: "Some night, huh? Some dinner, huh? Some house, huh? Some ugly baby, huh?"

At birth, New Life Christian church was not a pretty baby. We had dreamed of a gorgeous baby. We had worked hard for an attractive baby. We prayed for a good, healthy baby. Instead, we got a baby that only a mother could love.

In the gestation period, we imagined a baby born with a core of 50 to 100 people that would quickly grow, exceeding 200 in Sunday morning attendance by the end of the first year. This wasn't just our dream. It also was the dream imposed by the experts we read. They said, "Break 200 by the end of the first year, or most likely you never will." (To enhance your enjoyment of this story, insert Billy Joel's song, "Pressure," at this point.)

This also was the dream we believed God gave us. Living in the Washington, D.C., area where the population at the time was approaching 4 million and a county whose population would soon exceed 1 million, we thought, *It doesn't seem very God-honoring to start a church with the intention of being big enough to meet our needs and to pay the basic bills, so that we could have a comfortable place for us. In a growing metropolitan area like this, to be faithful means to reach as many people as possible as fast as possible.*

We dreamed that at birth our baby would boast the strength of multiple, paid staff members, including a church planter in residence. Again, this was not just our dream. We listened to the experts who said, "If a church doesn't start a new church within her first three years, she likely never will." ("Pressure!")

Once again, we believed this also was a godly mandate. Washington, D.C., is not just the capital of the United States. It is, as they say on local radio stations here, "the most powerful city in the world." The kingdom opportunity in Washington, however, is in sending, not keeping. Move to the city as an outsider like I did in 1987, and one of the first things you'll discover is that most people living here are not from here and many won't stay here long. (My wife is the exception. I did the research. Laura is one of only 17 people who grew up in this area and still lives here. Really.) If a church has a "scarcity," "holding tight" mentality, Washington, D.C. will drive you nutty. Once you embrace the opportunity of transience—the opportunity to love, to prepare, and then to send people—Washington becomes the ideal church-planting hub.

So before birth, we dreamed that we weren't just starting one church, but that this was the first of many churches. If God would so bless, we would not be a small church. Though small in number at birth, we would be a church-planting church of big impact that was just getting started.

Then the baby was born. April 1993. That year, the Chicago Cubs' dreams of breaking their World Series drought looked much more promising than the realization of our dreams. We were 15 core people, not 50. One staff member, not many. No church planter in training. No money. (Full disclosure: We had just $15,000 to cover marketing, a computer, sound equipment, and sundry other start-up fees. Brimming with cash, we were not.)

For months, we averaged 45 people on Sunday morning. Every week, half of our attendees were newcomers. Many Sundays after tearing down, Laura and I would sit in our car in the parking lot, breathing for the first time in hours. I would look at her and say the same thing, "45 again today. You know, if first-timers ever quit showing up, we're done." (Norman Vincent Peale, I was not.) Add to our list of frustrations that we had absolutely no momentum to reach 200 people by our first anniversary—something else we had dreamed about doing.

As we planted New Life in northern Virginia, Mark and Dee Dee Kitts were planting a church in North Carolina. Dee Dee was the first person I ever heard compare the work of church planting to the mythological Greek king, Sisyphus. According to legend, Sisyphus founded the ancient city that became known as Corinth. Sadly, pride and a proclivity for deception got the best of Sisyphus, and he messed with the wrong Greek gods once too often. He put the god Death in chains—and Death didn't like it. Inevitably, Death gets free and punishes Sisyphus with never-ending futility. For all eternity, Sisyphus is condemned to push a giant boulder to the top of a great mountain only to see the boulder roll back to the bottom each time he makes it to the top. The picture of futility.

Can you relate? In the first years of the new church, we felt Sisyphus' pain. In most new churches, the church planter is the momentum. It seems like where you move, the church moves; where you stop, the church stops. Every week, you push the boulder up the mountain. Every Sunday afternoon, you eat lunch feeling the reward that comes from reaching the top of the mountain, followed by feeling the burden to do it all over again. Push that boulder long enough, and eventually you begin to wonder, *Am I just* wasting my time? Is this worth the sacrifice? Were our dreams a mirage? Were these dreams God's, or ours?

Moments like this beg the Kipling question: Can you dream—and not make dreams your master?

Dreaming Through the Awkward Years

In her best-selling book, *Bird by Bird*, author Anne Lamott talks about the writing process and the misperceptions people have about writers:

> *"People tend to look at successful writers, writers who are getting their books published and maybe even doing well financially, and think that they sit down at their desks every morning feeling like a million dollars, feeling great about who they are and how much talent they have and what a great story they have to tell; that they take a few deep breaths, push back their sleeves, roll their necks a few times to get all the cricks out, and dive in, typing fully formed pages as fast as a court reporter. But this is just the fantasy of the uninitiated. I know some very great writers, writers you love who ... have made a great deal of money, and not one of them sits down routinely feeling wildly enthusiastic and confident. Not one of them writes elegant first drafts."*

I confess that I have a mythical image of an effective church planter. It parallels the image that most have of successful writers. If you're a planter, you know that most church planters don't wake up every day feeling giddy about who they are, the plans they make, the sermons they write, and the results they see. However, in the first years of church planting, that fantasy image of "church planter" beat me down like I was the Washington Redskins' defense playing Peyton Manning (or any quarterback, for that matter) every week.

In our second year as a church, our dreams looked like mist with no hope of ever being grasped. Then one night, Bob and Judy Russell took my wife and me to dinner. For over 30 years, Bob led Southeast Christian Church in Louisville, Kentucky. In his time there, the church became the largest in Kentucky and one of the largest in the country. Bob knew a thing or two about growing a healthy church. Fortunately for me, Bob's mom and my grandmother had been friends since Bob was an infant, so he had to be nice to me, or risk trouble with his mom.

Over dinner, I shared our woes: "We've dreamed! We've tried! Nothing's happening! No momentum! No church planter! No money!" Bob listened patiently then responded with classic Russell candor: "Brett, give God some credit. Maybe, God knows what He's doing. Maybe, God is giving you everything and everyone you can handle right now."

That wasn't what I wanted to hear. I wanted Bob to say, "Brett, if you just make a couple minor adjustments, all your dreams will come true!" I wanted to hear, "Brett, with a hefty influx of cash from a megachurch in Louisville, the sky's the limit!" I wouldn't have minded hearing, "Brett, that a handsome, athletic, multi-talented guy like you is so under-appreciated is cosmically criminal! It is further proof of just how fallen our world is!"

I also wanted to argue with God: Perhaps He was underestimating my capacity? If God is giving me all I can be faithful with, surely He just didn't understand that I was eager to handle more people, more baptisms, more impact, more money, more church plants, and more influence *right now*! I really didn't want to hear, "Maybe God knows what He's doing. Maybe God is building the church His way." But that's what I needed to hear.

How did the wisest man in the Old Testament word it? "Trust in the Lord with all your heart. Don't lean on your own understanding" (Prov. 3:5). Yes, that's what I needed to hear.

Chastised, but encouraged, we returned to our toddler church. Looking back, I realize we had let the dream become our master. One of the dangerous things about kingdom work is that you can do good things for bad reasons and die spiritually while leaving a beautiful body of work. This is Jesus' warning to the church of Ephesus in Revelation 2. First, carefully read Jesus' words of praise, and imagine how pleased you would be to hear Him speak those words to your church this Sunday:

"I know your works, your labor, your patience, and that you cannot bear those who are evil. And you have tested those who say they are apostles and are not, and have found them liars; and you have persevered and have patience, and have labored for My name's sake and have not become weary."

Impressive praise, until you read the rest of the story:

"Nevertheless I have this against you, that you have left your first love. Remember therefore from where you have fallen; repent and do the first works, or else I will come to you quickly and remove your lampstand from its place— unless you repent."

That is what it looks like when a church lets dreams become the master. Dreams are pursued and achieved. Awards are won. People do good things. Leaders receive accolades and recognition. But hearts are not right. Good dreams are pursued; they just aren't God-dreams. Good things are accomplished, just not for God's honor and with God's power. This is what happens when the dream is the master, not God. You love the dream more than you love Him. You love the idea of church planting more than the

Creator. Just as Jesus called the church in Ephesus to repent, He called me to repent.

True story. A Chinese minister recently visited the United States. He visited several megachurches. On his way to catch his return flight to China, his host asked the minister, "After visiting all these megachurches in America, what did you learn? What one lesson surprised you most?"

His answer stunned his host: "It is amazing how much the church in America can accomplish without the power of God."

In other words, this minister saw a church of style over substance. We are long on strategies and methods, but short on prayer and power. This is what it looks like when dreams become your master. We were clearly traveling this road before Bob said, "Give God some credit. Maybe He knows what He's doing."

I'm still not sure I know what it means to let God build the church, but we returned from that meeting renewed in our commitment to make that our quest. If the dream is His dream, we don't pursue the dream; we pursue Him. We don't create the dream; we seek His face. We don't make it happen; we follow His leading. We don't put our hope in our dreams; we put our hope in God.

Two practical applications immediately became clear. First, we needed to talk with God more; second, we needed to quit fretting about what we didn't have and start focusing more on being faithful with the resources God had already given us.

This immediately led to two action points. First, we were inspired to pray more. Rick Stedman, a church-planting friend in California, tells a powerful story about prayer. Like just about every children's ministry, his church's children's ministry struggled to recruit enough volunteers. Naturally, Rick's staff regularly expressed frustration. Finally one day, he responded, "Whose church is it anyway?" he asked them. "Is it ours, or is it God's?" (Some would call this a rhetorical question. I call this a "so simple why-didn't-I-think-of-it" question.) Rick continued: "If it's God's church, then to whom are we talking more? To God or to people? Who are you asking more for help? God or people?"

As we put more trust in God to build our church, we found ourselves asking Rick's question a lot, "Whose church is it? Who are you talking to about it?"

Second, we started intentionally looking for ways in which God was already at work, building the church and teaching us to trust Him. For instance, our first worship leader, Joe—the Babe Ruth of worship leaders (if Babe Ruth sported a guitar and a pony tail)—was literally an answer to prayer. One day, I prayed for a worship leader; that week a friend put me in touch with Joe. (That kind of thing may happen to you every hour; not to me.) People adored Joe. When asked why they attended New Life, most people noted "the music" first—not "the preaching!" So, when Joe told us he wanted to go on tour our second summer, every emotion screamed, "Noooo," but we knew better. (Whose church is it? God's church, or my church? Who are we trusting to provide?) So, we released Joe to serve away from us for a season.

That summer, God did more than we could have asked or imagined. He provided "Air Force Guy." To this day, no one remembers his name. But a few weeks before Joe's tour began, "Air Force Guy" showed up asking, "Do you need any help with your worship team?" Like the homely geek being asked to the prom by the beauty queen, we said, "Sure do!" All summer he led worship—great worship. Then, the week after Joe returned from his tour, "Air Force Guy" left, transferred out of the state. My wife calls him "the angel man." (I suspect he was from Atlantis.) He was an answer to prayer, and God was teaching us to hold things, people and dreams loosely. As Laura says,

"Unless you give God a chance to provide, how is He going to?"

The Stretch of the Dream
Few people had more influence on the church-planting scene of the late 20th century than Robert Logan. In his *Church Planter's Toolkit* resource, he asks a question that has often served as a North Star of sorts to give us direction in uncertain times. I suspect every multiplying church has asked the question in some form through the years. Specifically, "If you could do anything for the glory of God and know that it wouldn't fail, what would you do?" Ponder that question. Answer it. Then, ask yourself the buzzer-beater question: "Why don't you do it?"

Our core team started New Life Christian Church with the conviction that obedience to God meant we would be a church-planting church. As I mentioned earlier, we weren't starting one church; we were starting the first church of many. One need not be a card-carrying Mensa member to deduce that if we were going to be a church-planting church, eventually we would need to plant a church.

Were we ready? We had less than 100 people. Our annual budget (if you could call it that) was less than $75,000. Somehow, we had saved $10,000. We had no plan. No real strategy. I was 28 years old and had one year of church-planting experience. What more does a new church need to be ready?

In Joshua 3, God prepares the people of Israel to cross the Jordan River on dry land before taking the Promised Land. Future generations will leverage this moment to teach their children that the God they serve is powerful and worthy of wholehearted trust. As the story goes, God not only stopped the waters so the people could pass over on dry ground, but He stopped the waters upstream, "a great distance away at Adam," ten or eleven miles upstream.

When we looked to plant a church out of our church, all we could see were the limited resources in front of us. We had no idea about all the work God had been doing upstream to prepare us for the journey ahead.

Upstream, God brought Vince Antonnuci to northern Virginia. Three years before we started New Life, Vince was a pre-law student who had just become a Christian at my sister's church in Buffalo, New York. Six months after being baptized, Vince moved to Alexandria, Virginia, for a brief internship in D.C. When Vince moved, my sister called, hoping I might be able to connect with him. But Washington is a big area. What were the chances Vince would be anywhere close to us? When God is working upstream, the chances are pretty good. It turned out that Vince was living in an apartment walking- distance from our condo.

After moving away from D.C., Vince kept in touch. Passionate about Jesus, he dropped out of a full ride at law school so he could pursue vocational ministry. As New Life started, Vince was working as an intern at a megachurch. Soon, his internship would finish. That church was offering him a good salary with a high-profile opportunity.

Instincts told me that Vince would make a stud church planter, but I knew it made no sense for him to join us. He could either stay with a high-visibility megachurch and get paid a healthy salary or move to a small, struggling, invisible church, take a pay cut, and raise two-thirds of his salary. He could stay and live in a Midwestern city with a low cost of living, or move and live in an eastern city with one of the highest costs of living in the country.

Perhaps asking would be an exercise in futility, but James 4:3 says, "you have not because you ask not", so I asked God, and then Vince. Like a scene out of *Dumb and*

Dumber, Vince said, "Not in a million years," to which I replied, "So, you're telling me there's a chance!"

Vince and his wife Jennifer flew out for a weekend. Before the weekend was over, Jennifer looked at him and said, "Vince, this is where you need to be. This is where you will make the biggest difference."

That weekend, God was teaching all of us something about how He builds the church. Not by might. Not by power. Vince wasn't impressed by our preaching, our organization, or our size. He was impressed by a clear sense of God's calling. God's dream is not limited by our ability (or inability) to pay high-quality staff. Call the called. If they are called and listening to God's lead, pay won't matter. If they're not called or not listening, you don't want to pay them enough to catch them anyway.

Like manna in the wilderness, Vince and Jennifer were God's perfect provision to meet our need in that season of our journey. For the first time since starting New Life, I could see God answer our prayers, bringing a solid team together to bring the dream to life. Joe was the loveable, gracious, amazingly talented worship stud. Vince was the high-energy, creative, risk-taker. And I was the "steady-as-she-goes," button-down collar planter. We had a solid team that was going places! And before long, two out of three of us did.

Holding the Dream Tight; Letting Friends Go

I knew the day was coming when I would leave my daughter, Emily, at college. It was a day we looked forward to for years. Her situation could not have been better. She was at University of Virginia, she had great roommates, great courses, a great situation in every way. Yet, I dreaded the moment. The "goodbye." Laura and Emily hugged like mature human beings. Emily turned to me for a hug. If the girls in the next room heard the next sound, surely they must have wondered if Emily was hiding a baby pig. It was not the most masculine moment of my life by far. A significant new chapter for Emily needed to begin. I was thrilled, and it made me weep.

I knew the day was coming when Vince said, "Brett, I think its time for us to plant." From the start, that was the dream. For this reason, Vince was brought on staff. Mentally, spiritually, and rationally, I fully embraced the dream. Emotionally, it tore me up.

"Brett," Vince continued, "I've talked to Joe. I'd really like him to go with us to plant in Virginia Beach."

Well, I hadn't seen that coming. I did not agree. The fight with God was on! *Lord, is this Your idea or just a bad idea? Either way, I don't appreciate it! Look, I hate to see Vince and Jennifer go. But, I get it. That's my selfish self-resisting. But Joe? At least leave Joe!*

I continued: *Vince is not replaceable, Lord. I've never known anyone in ministry quite like him. I'll give you him.* (I'm sure God was impressed by my magnanimity). *But, how will a church our size ever replace Joe? Come on, Lord! Vince AND Joe! That's two-thirds of our staff!*

Everyone who has ever wrestled with God discovers the same reality: It is not a winnable wrestling match. (Or, perhaps, it's one you always win?) Joe and Vince were headed to the beach, and with them, I feared, were our dreams.

I remember sharing my fears with Marj Furgerson. She had become like a second mom to me when I moved to Washington. Sitting in her family room one dark afternoon, I voiced my fears, "Marj, I don't know if New Life will ever grow again now that Vince and Joe are planting. You just can't replace Vince and Joe. And, yet, I know the only thing more risky than following God is disobeying Him because we want to play it safe."

Dream Faithfulness. Dream Foolishness
I grew up water-skiing. By my senior year in high school, I prided myself for being above average. My oldest brother, Phil, however, was seven years older and seven years better. Living in Tennessee, he skied competitively, year round. That summer, I looked forward to impressing my big brother. This would also be my chance to get a few tips from the pro. That day, I felt like I'd skied like the next Bob LaPoint. Crawling into the back of the boat afterward, I asked, "Well, Phil, what do I need to learn? How can I improve?"

His response was classic older brother: "There's so much. I wouldn't know where to begin."

After sending Vince and Joe to start ForeFront in Virginia Beach, we knew we had a lot to learn about church planting. Immediately, one lesson rose to the top: The people who were most involved in the new church work were also the ones who developed the strongest vision for church planting. Of course, to some degree they learned the most because they were the most teachable—that's why they were quick to commit in the first place. But we were also convinced (and still are to this day) that the more closely involved people were in the church plant, the more they got to see lost people saved, so the more passionate they became to start more churches.

The Sunday we announced the opening day attendance for ForeFront, we also announced our commitment to plant our next new church. Two questions drove our philosophy for the next plant: 1) How do we involve more New Lifers and ignite passion for church planting? 2) What does it mean to plant a church like Matthew 25 faithful stewards?

Since starting New Life, Jesus' parable of the stewards in Matthew 25 kept hitting us in the face. In the story, the master goes on a journey, entrusting three managers with his wealth. One manager receives five talents, another receives two talents, and another receives just one. Each one gets something. All are expected to be faithful. When the master returns, he praises managers one and two, "Well done. You have been faithful over little. I will set you over much."

No doubt, manager three expected to hear the same praise. After all, he hadn't squandered the wealth in "riotous living." He hadn't spent it on a vacation. He hadn't gambled it on something stupid like the Redskins having a decent season. He had just played it safe. How stunned manager three must have been to hear the master utter the words, "You wicked, lazy servant. You ought to have known me better! You should have done something with the talent I gave you!"

How stunned Jesus' crowd must have been when He turned to them and said, "For everyone who has more will be given, and he will have an abundance. But from the one who has not, even what he has will be taken away."

With ForeFront planted, we asked ourselves that question, "What does it mean for us to be a Matthew 25 church-planting church?" Obviously, the answer was "risk." The pesky implication of Matthew 25 is that faithful stewards don't just risk a fraction of the talents they've been given, or even a safe portion; they risk every talent. "Does that mean," we continued to ask, "to be a Matthew 25 church planting church, we must be willing to risk losing everything?"

In his famous poem, *The Hollow Men*, T.S. Eliot captures our fears:

Between the idea
And the reality
Between the motion
And the act
Falls the Shadow
For Thine is the Kingdom

Reading Matthew 25 dispassionately, it's easy to buzz past "the Shadow." If you're not careful, Jesus' story reads like a math equation: Received talents plus risked talents equals doubled talents. Simple. Straightforward. Inevitable.

However, to dare to live the equation is to discover that moving beyond the plus sign means driving through a dark tunnel. T.S. Eliot calls this tunnel, "the Shadow." It is that season after you've released all the talents, when the win is far from certain. It is in the dark where the risk becomes real and all can be lost. It is the season after the emotion of the conception has faded when the responsibility for the risks wears down the dreamer.

What happened in "the Shadow" after the managers risked all their talents, as they awaited a return on their faithfulness? Like Joseph's 13 years in prison in Egypt, was it a time of confusion? Like Job's 39 chapters of pain and loss, did they ever wonder why God felt so silent? So distant? Or, like Dietrich Bonhoeffer facing the noose, were they at peace knowing their victory was in their faithfulness, even if it looked like defeat to most? Eliot continues:

> *Between the conception*
> *And the creation*
> *Between the emotion*
> *And the response*
> *Falls the Shadow*

For us, after starting ForeFront, Matthew 25 meant entering the shadow. Out next step was to church plant in a way that put everything at risk. Talents could be doubled, or all could be lost.

Into the Shadow of the Dream

"There are known knowns. These are things we know that we know. There are known unknowns. That is to say, there are things that we know we don't know. But there are also unknown unknowns. There are things we don't know we don't know."—Former U.S. Secretary of Defense Donald Rumsfeld's response when questioned about the lack of evidence linking the Iraq government with the supply of weapons of mass destruction to terrorist groups

Today, over 5,000 churches consider themselves multisite in America. When we began exploring "Matthew 25" church planting, fewer than 100 churches were multisite. Friends of ours, Dave and Jon Ferguson at Community Christian Church in Chicago, were pioneering multisite, inviting us to join them for the ride. The risk was obvious. The price of pioneering is usually the life of the pioneer.

We knew to start a new church as a campus could cost us dearly. We were a moderate-sized church of 600. We had some momentum, but not like a church of 2,000. We had some systems developed, but nothing approaching the complexity necessary to be a healthy multisite church. Multisite was either a bold step of faith, or it was outpunting our coverage. On the "release talents" side of the equation, we weren't smart enough to know which was true.

Hockey great Wayne Gretzky once said, "You miss 100 percent of the shots you don't take." That's how we felt about multisite. The opportunity promised too much not to take a shot. We could start a church with the maturity of an existing church; we could expand geographically, while focusing locally; and we could get bigger (reaching more people), while also getting better (in quality). Above all, we knew it would stretch us as a church like nothing else had—and if the church plant did not go well, she would drag us down like ten anchors from a rowboat.

Step one: Hire Wayne Gretzky. If you're going to take your best shot, it's a good idea to have "The Great One" on your team. One thing every multisite church had in common in those early days was a Wayne Gretzky. They all had at least one organizational "great one" developing strategies and managing complexities.

Now, for years, I had done my best to beg, cajole, manipulate and blackmail Todd Wilson (yes, Exponential Director Todd Wilson) to come into ministry. Todd was a nuclear engineer in the NavSea, the nuclear Navy. In my associate ministry (when God was preparing the dream upstream), Todd and his wife Anna worked as volunteers in our youth ministry. In 1992, Todd moved to Maine to oversee the Portsmouth Naval Shipyard where he was told, "Few people in the history of the program have your promotion record." Todd was on the fast track, being prepared to lead the nuclear Navy someday. But, I knew Todd's heart for God. As a preacher, I thought, "Nuclear engineer. Fast-track promotion record in the nuclear Navy. Obviously, God's preparing this guy for ministry!"

Todd captured God's vision for ministry and joined us to lead the charge into multisite. His first question to me was, "So, how do we start a new church?" Before starting New Life, I bought poster board and Post-It notes. On each Post-It note, I wrote a specific job to be done, a goal to be achieved, or a deadline to reach. Although my poster board provided more than enough detail for a guy with a preaching degree, it seemed a tad insufficient for the nuclear engineer trained in "assume it wrong, prove it right," and an organizational culture where back-up systems required back-up systems with back-up systems one hundred layers deep.

"When New Life began," I told Todd, "I didn't know if I had the right answers. Even scarier for me, I was always haunted by the reality that I wasn't even asking the right questions!" To use Donald Rumsfeld's language, we planted New Life "living in the unknown unknowns."

With that thought, Todd went to work uncovering the unknowns and by the time he had finished, he had compiled a process for church planting—a series of questions, really. Something like 3,014 questions (okay, it was actually more like 500 questions, but I was lost after the first 10). These were basic questions, designed to help us discover our essential unknowns. Working those questions, our church, New Life—Dulles, launched with 414 people on the first Sunday.

And we lived happily ever after.

No. That would be too boring. As surely as the miracles of Acts 2 and 3 are followed by the arrests of Acts 4, the Ananias and Sapphira of Acts 5, and the squabbling of Acts 6, the thrill of every church plant is followed by a shadow.

Our shadow began with a desertion. If anyone ever asks, "What is it like to start a brand new church without a church planter?" we can answer that question. We should have seen it coming. No one is more to blame than I am for not being more perceptive and responsible. Three months before launch, our church planter was showing signs of wear. Perhaps, we didn't prepare him well enough. Certainly, we placed him in a role that exceeded his capacity. Yet, at this point, the ship had already sailed. We agreed to launch the church and then make adjustments later.

A month before launch, after months of building a core team, after $30,000 had been spent on postcards and thousands more had been invested in outreach events, our planter bailed. Author and organizational expert Warren Bennis says that the footprints of the leader are seen all over the organization. My footprints were all over this disaster, but there was no time for licking wounds or pointing fingers. We had a shadow to plow through.

Like first-time parents trying to learn how to parent on the fly, we groped our way through our first years of multisite. In the first five years, the Dulles campus would share six campus pastors, move four times, and struggle to maintain any momentum. Four hundred turned into three hundred, until we settled around two hundred people on Sunday mornings. (So, if you need know-how for leading a church from four hundred to two hundred, we got that covered.)

More Than We Can See
Leadership 101 teaches us, "What gets measured, gets done." True, but it's a tricky truth. How do you measure how God builds a dream? When do you measure when God is at work? God had a dream for Abraham: "I'm going to make you a great nation." Abraham measured the development of the dream, assessed inadequate progress, and took action. The Middle East has been at war ever since.

We believed God gave New Life Christian a dream: Be a church-planting church to reach as many people as possible as fast as possible in Chantilly, Virginia, Washington D.C., and throughout the world. We sacrificed our best staff to start a church in Virginia Beach to be faithful to the dream. Now, we were taking a Matthew 25 risk to start a new church in a new way in Dulles. Imagine our disappointment when two years later, it felt like we were failing, not growing. The new church was struggling, and our original campus—for the first time in her story—was stagnant. While our growth was never dramatic in Chantilly, it was always consistent. The resource drag and distraction of the new church was pulling down the entire church.

Had we made mistakes? Yes. Had we been over confident? I'm sure. Would better leaders have navigated the stormy waters more deftly? Absolutely. But where in

Matthew 25 does Scripture indicate that faithful stewardship means perfect stewardship? If God only doubles the talents of perfect leaders, why didn't the apostle Paul, the worst of sinners, abandon all hope? Reflecting on Paul's self-assessment, a friend once observed that if we don't think we are the worst of sinners, we're not very aware of the ugliness of our sins.

So while we were not perfect, we soldiered on, confident that God hadn't released us from the dream, yet. Today, fifteen years removed from that shadow season, we see more clearly that our dreams were good, but God's dreams were great. While we were working on the dreams we could physically see, God was at work on dreams that were more than we could have asked or imagined. While we dreamed of starting a new church to reach people in Dulles, God was developing ministries to help start many churches that would reach people throughout the world. While our dream was to see our talents doubled in northern Virginia, God was at work multiplying His talents nationally.

What happened? Since New Life was a mobile church that disappeared six days a week, we regularly used marketing cards to help our people start spiritual conversations with their neighbors. Starting the Dulles campus forced us to market smarter. This led other churches to ask us for help, which led to starting a church marketing non-profit that directly and indirectly helped hundreds of new churches get started.

Helping new churches with marketing led us to a scary discovery. There is something worse than a small opening day—a large opening day in a church unprepared to give birth! It's axiomatic that it's easier to reach people the first time than to reach them again after a negative experience. Through church marketing, we were helping churches reach a crowd when the more essential need was to help them be healthy.

Suddenly, Todd's three thousand essential questions for starting a church moved beyond being just a good idea to help us start the Dulles campus. At this point, we asked church planting organization leaders around the nation, "Does anyone offer project management assistance for church planters?" Everyone we asked said, "No! And, it is desperately needed!"

This is how *Converge*, an online, church-planting project management guide, came to life. *Converge* became the primary tool for Passion for Planting, our project management service that shepherds church planters from church conception to church birth. Thousands of new churches have used our free resources. Dozens have been started using our project managers or managers that we've released.

And, then, there's Todd Wilson. After Todd joined our staff, I often thought, *If we had tried to hold onto Vince when we needed to release him, I wonder if God would have ever entrusted us with Todd?* Follow that reasoning long enough, and it lands you at one logical conclusion: Whatever dream God has for us next means that one day we will release Todd for greater kingdom impact. Today, Todd continues to serve on New Life staff, but as our missionary for church planting. Most of his time and energy is dedicated to leading Exponential's church planting efforts.

Was God faithful when we attempted to be a Matthew 25, talent-risking, church-planting church? Did He double the talents? Not as we dreamed He would. Not in the way we could see. But, yes, in ways far beyond our ability to ask or imagine. If He could multiply our talents, He can certainly do even more through you, if you dare to let Him.

Chapter 2
Tensions in Multiplication

1. Addition (Attendance Growth) vs. Multiplication (Start New Places of Growth)
Admittedly, pride is my greatest struggle. It is my biggest problem, my greatest hindrance, as a church planter. Now, it requires no self-awareness for me to admit that. The same is true for you, your spouse, your best friend, and your worst enemy. In his seminal work, *Mere Christianity*, C.S. Lewis called pride "the essential vice, the utmost evil."

In elementary school, pride meant that I dreamed of being the star point guard, carried off the court after sinking the District 10 Championship winning shot. Call it natural ambition, childhood narcissism, or a congenital drive for parental approval—pride drives me to make me the star of the story. As a church planter, the primary reason I feel tension between addition and multiplication is how it makes me feel about me. Addition makes me the star point guard winning the game. Multiplication means I become more like John the Baptizer: Jesus increases while I decrease.

To weed out my heart, I must constantly ask, "Does the church exist to make me feel good about myself, or so that God's name can be lifted up? Is my work in the kingdom just my sick, pseudo-spiritual pursuit of the American dream?"

I wonder how much the "addition vs. multiplication" tension inside me would disappear if I had the heart of Mary, Jesus' mother. What an honor to be chosen by God to give birth to His Son! As she rocked her baby to sleep, what vision she must have seen for her preferable future! How her Son would be worshipped as the Redeemer of Israel! How He would be highly regarded by the Highly Regarded! How He would make their family's name great! How proud she would be to watch Him grow and then take over the family business! How secure she would feel, knowing He would be by her side, caring for her in her twilight years.

Then, one day, her dreams walk out the door. The One she gave birth to follows a path she had not envisioned. He shows more interest in sacrificial service than making a name for the family. He doesn't impress the impressive people. He doesn't even care to build a place to rest His own head.

Then, one day, her dream dies. Mary's dreams for Jesus died a hundred ways in the three years after He left home, but how final this death felt. How the words of Simeon resonated that day, "... and a sword will pierce your own soul too."

For us, "addition vs. multiplication" is a matter of the heart. Can I dream and not make dreams my master? Like Mary, we have been entrusted with God's dream. We can dream about the dream, but we're not entitled to our dream. It is not our dream. It is not our baby.

If I were ever to kill my pride long enough, the "addition vs. multiplication" tension might not get simple, but at least it would be clear. One primary responsibility of the leader is to apply finite resources to the critical growth path. Of course, God's resources are infinite, but the resources we're entrusted with are limited. The tension of addition vs. multiplication resolves when the focus becomes this singular question: How can we impact the most people the most effectively?

As always, Jesus is our perfect example. Jesus had no "addition/multiplication" bifurcation. Remember how He invested His time? He spent isolated time in prayer, personal time with the twelve, private time with the three, and public time with the crowds. He divided His time, but not His focus. Measured by results two thousand years later, He invested every moment focused on one goal, "that the world may know" the Father sent Him.

What would it look like in your church if every decision made answered the question, "How does this move the ball forward for the greatest kingdom impact?" Practically, we've found clarity seeking the harmony of three questions:

1) What is best for the individual?
2) What is best for the congregation?
3) What is best for the kingdom?

Often, we'll reverse the order and weigh the answers. For instance, emotionally, it's not easy to release a Todd Wilson. Just think of the impact he could have adding to New Life if his energies were focused on northern Virginia! However, that only addresses question No. 2.

What's best for Todd, according to whom God has called and created him to be? God has given Todd a uniquely creative mind. Every time Todd mowed his lawn, he finished with fresh ideas for a new 501c3, a new national ministry that could unleash previously untapped kingdom potential. Listen to ideas like that long enough, what's best for Todd (question No. 1) and the kingdom (question No. 3) becomes clear. When two out of three become clear, the answer to the third question either clarifies, or it exposes your selfish motives that hinder you from coming to clarity.

2. Facility Acquisition v. Facility Sacrifice
Most people can be lazy. Even the most driven among us usually prefer the path of least resistance. So, we need motivation to exercise, to diet, to finish a degree, to pursue a goal, or to overcome an addiction. In one area of my life, I've never needed motivation—selfishness. Remarkably,

I've never needed a better book or conference on how to order my life more proficiently around me. Isn't that the natural bent of every organization, as well? Few organizations need to hire a specialist for "how to be more focused on us!" That's why in the church it's always easier to find a champion to "take care of us" than champions for those who are far from God.

With that understanding of reality, we made several decisions when New Life was young. First, since others will naturally champion the internal focus, I would always be the champion for reaching as many people as possible as fast as possible. Second, we would live out our commitment to church planting (our ultimate application of the focus on reaching lost people) through two financial commitments: 1) Our missions giving will focus on church planting (today, the first twelve percent of our total budget goes to church planting). 2) We would not build for ourselves until we started a church for others.

Jesus taught, "Where your treasure is, there your heart will be also" (Matt. 6:21). The relationship is more symbiotic than linear. Heart follows treasure, and treasure follows heart. For us, facility was a matter of heart and trust. We wanted a heart that placed God and others first, not ourselves. So we trusted that in time, God would prove Himself faithful and take care of our facility needs.

Of course, He did. But, He did not provide as we had hoped. Author and pastor Tim Keller observes, "Christianity doesn't give you what you want, it is more like an explosion that destroys everything you had to make way for something new."

That is our church-planting story. That is our building story.

We dreamed. God delayed. Our dreams died. We grew confused. Some people doubted. Some people quit. It was not fun. Then, God provided a greater dream. We call it the nZone (thenzone.com). It is an 83,000-square-foot, seven-day-a-week, full-service sports facility. In the average year, 400,000 people will use the building—most of which do not consider themselves New Lifers. On one hand, the poorest young people in the community use it for free weekly. On the other hand, professional athletes use it to condition in the off-season. Before opening the nZone, we prayed for a building that would make an unbelieving community thankful for the church. Since opening, we have received more community service awards than ever, and the praise of the county zoning board.

Here's the most important point: If New Life had tried to build sooner, we never would have developed the vision for the outreach ministries at the nZone. If we had pushed for "a place for us" sooner, the timing would have been wrong, and we never would have had the financial capacity to afford the nZone. By focusing on reaching others through church planting first, we did not sacrifice anything, really. Because we focused on church planting first, God made our vineyard more abundantly fruitful when the time was right.

3. New Campus (Multisite) vs. New Plant (Multiplication)

Where were you September 11, 2001? It's one of those days emblazoned on everyone's memory. I was in Naperville, Illinois, attending a multisite symposium organized by Naperville Community Christian Church. The conference gathered multisite churches and churches considering multisite. That year, we had started a campus multisite as a church-planting strategy—not as an overflow room, or a way to showcase the preacher, or as an acquisition of a church in decline. At the symposium, we felt out of place. Rare was the multisite campus started as a church-planting motive.

In the years ahead, we added two more campuses. The first was a new work. The second was a dying church, asking us for a lifeline. Over time, a strange thing happened: We quit asking the right questions. When New Life was young and organized simply, every murky decision was answered with one clarifying question, "What's the best way to reach lost people?" After several years of being multisite, one day it dawned on me, "I have changed my questions!" After becoming multisite, we became obsessed with questions like, "How is a multisite church supposed to be organized?" and "Are we taking advantage of economies of scale?" and "Who is ultimately responsible for that problem?" In other words, we were no longer focused on the questions that lead to long-term multiplication; we had become focused on organizational self-perpetuation questions.

While some churches have been able to defeat that monster, it wasn't a battle we felt called to fight. We decided we were called to simplify and refocus. So, we have released two campuses and function as a two-campus church. Today, we church plant in networks, through individual plants. Eventually, we may even church plant as a short-term campus. But the sideways energy required to be a multisite beyond two campuses does not produce the return on investment we have found with individual autonomy.

Rare is the multisite church with campuses that exceed the original campus in size and speed of growth. Why? I don't know. But in view of our desire for multiplication over addition, that "why" question needs to be pondered.

4. The Planter Tension: Highly Prepared vs. Spiritually Empowered

If there is one Rorschach test for church-planting leaders, this is it. Where a group or individual lands on this tension says more about them than about the tension. We at New Life have failed in both directions, I'm sure.

When New Life started, I wasn't ready. If I had gone through an assessment center, I'm sure I would have failed. I was over-confident and under-prepared. As a result, I fear we have allowed the expectation pendulum to swing to the opposite extreme. We rarely say, "This is perfect. Perfect person. Perfect preparation. Perfect timing. Perfect match." Most of the time, after prayer and the wisdom of a multitude of counselors, we agree, "This person is roughly right, roughly ready."

We use the same tools (interviews, references, online assessments, assessment centers) that everyone else uses to make sure someone is roughly ready. If God is readying us to release someone for multiplication, we have learned to watch for one other critical indicator, as well. In nature, to get her babies to leave the nest, a mother bird will make the nest uncomfortable. In the home, God prepares parents to release their young adult children by making the nest uncomfortable. In the church, God disturbs the nest, as well.

For instance, Vince is a gifted preacher, a crazy creative thinker, and visionary. Vince needed to preach every week. Vince needed to be able to pursue his creative ideas more aggressively. He needed the freedom to lead a church that reflected the personality and gifts God gave him. How sinful it would have been for me to think, *Vince needs to ratchet down his aggressiveness!* Vince was made to turn the world upside-down. He deserved to be respected and released. But in the process, his growth made the nest uncomfortable.

By the way, so much unnecessary conflict could be diffused if we saw this discomfort through God's eyes of building the church, and not our eyes, trying to control it.

The same story could be told for each of the church planters we have trained and released. Part of me would have enjoyed keeping each of them on the team. Each was gifted. Each created a following in the church. Each brought a unique personality to the staff that the church never replaced after they left to plant. Yet, each was too strong and gifted to be confined to our nest. I thank the Lord that He creates discomfort in the nest; otherwise, we might find it easier to keep everyone at home.

Chapter 3
We Messed Up,
So You Don't Have To

At the risk of stating the absurdly obvious, church planters don't know what we don't know. How can our churches move from addition to multiplication? How can we invest our time, treasure and talents for the greatest kingdom return in one hundred years from now? If we're honest (and have a skosh of humility), we will admit the absurdly obvious: There is more in that universe of wisdom that we don't know than we do know.

    A leadership coach once pointed out to me that the first step of growth is moving from unconscious incompetence to conscious incompetence. Twenty years after starting New Life, most days I still don't feel competent; however, we have discovered a handful of watershed issues that can make or break us.

    If you're unfamiliar with a watershed, imagine watching two drops of rain fall in the Allegheny Mountains at the Chesapeake watershed. Theoretically, the two raindrops may fall inches away from each other, yet hundreds of miles later one will end up in the Gulf of Mexico while the other ends up in the Atlantic Ocean.

    Twenty years ago, we were mostly unconsciously incompetent regarding these issues. Today, we're aware that how we live out these issues will determine what kind of church we will be in the future. Fall on one side of the issue, in one hundred years from now we will be an "addition" impact church. Fall on the other side, in one hundred years we have a shot at being a "multiplication" impact church.

To be clear, we don't claim to have achieved competence with these issues; we're just glad to be aware of their vital nature. The battle is always fluid.

Watershed Issue #1: Whose Church Is it Anyway?
Knowledge is a funny thing. Baseball coaches, for instance, come in two forms. Some know baseball abstractly. Others know baseball in theory and in practice. I once watched an All-Star coach ride his son for striking out. His frustration seemed a bit disproportionate to the situation, but he was coaching an All-Star team. The pressure was on, and perhaps his shoes were too tight. At the next practice, all became clear. For fun, the coaches joined the players for a homerun-hitting context. Guess who could not hit a softly tossed pitch? Guess who looked like the only baseball he had ever hit was on his PlayStation? No wonder Coach Hothead was so frustrated with his son's hitting; this coach had no personal appreciation of how difficult it is to hit a rapidly moving round ball with a round bat.

"Whose church is it?" In the abstract, every Sunday school child knows how to answer that question. Jesus said, "I will build my church." Paul said, "I planted. Apollos watered. God made it grow." In other places in Scripture, Paul adds that Jesus is the head of the church and that He gave up His life to purchase the church with His precious blood. We all know it, but how often do church planters settle for "addition" because they know who builds the church the same way that Coach Hothead knows how to hit a baseball?

Now, of course, there are some who would use God's ownership of the church as their excuse not to accept responsibility. It is possible to resolve the issue by saying, "It's all God's, so I'm just going to hang out at Starbucks six days a week, enjoy my cup of joe, play Sudoku, convince myself that I'm pastoring my lost-but-caffeinated flock, and write off all losses to God." C.S. Lewis once observed that God gets blamed for many things He has nothing to do with. For some, blaming God for what He has nothing to do with is a personal philosophy of ministry. If a planter's vision is for "subtraction" in the next one hundred years, this approach is ideal.

     Most church planters wrestle with the other extreme: Hyper-ownership. We plan. We plant. We work. We fast. We build teams. We become the momentum. We enjoy the rewards; we suffer the losses, personally. It's our vision, our flock. And, any fingers point straight at us. This is the nature of ownership. This is normal. It's not all bad, but it's not all good, either. If left unchecked, this is toxic for the planter and for the church. Hyper-ownership makes us miserly and self-serving. Whatever multiplication DNA God might create in our ministry and us, hyper-ownership kills it.

     How might someone position himself on the healthy side of this issue? How can I own the church without possessing it? Like David, I have to constantly ask God to search me, to see if there is any untoward ways in me. Who do I believe grows the church? God or me? When there's trouble, whom do I turn to first? God, or others? Whose wisdom do I seek first? Whose power am I trusting more?

- **Who owns the church? Do I really trust in God for His wisdom, or do I trust in mine?**

     Thirty years ago, I heard a church-planting leader teach on the latest developments in church planting. Oozing sophomoric confidence, he said, "Our years of experience have taught us how to church plant almost scientifically. Today, we know how to find the right planter, how to prepare the planter, and how to plan the church plant for almost assured success."

     It was one of those moments when you hope that the distance between you and the speaker exceeds the power of the discharge of the lightning bolt that is certain to strike. All too often, that is the spirit of church planting: We have it all figured out. Just read the right books, attend enough conferences, apply the hippest strategy, and you can plant a successful church!

If we genuinely believe the church is God's church and that He builds His church, that means we genuinely believe 2 Timothy 3:16-17: "All Scripture is given by inspiration of God, and is profitable for doctrine, for reproof, for correction, for instruction in righteousness, that the man of God may be complete, thoroughly equipped for every good work."

Now, intellectuals scoff that this is naïve (because they know so much, you see) Liberals mock that this is simplistic; we have advanced beyond the primitive principles of Scripture (C.S. Lewis labeled this thinking, "chronological arrogance"). Yet, if we're going to let God build the church, the first essential is that we renew our confidence in His Word. Yes, His Word is living and active! Yes, if you ask biblical questions and seek to apply biblical principles, God will lead you to build His church in His way for His glory.

Space does not permit me to share the nZone story in detail, but our seven-day-a-week athletic space is a living example of how God builds the church when you seek His wisdom. Before building, we asked three biblical questions:

1) How can we best fulfill the Great Commission through a building (Matt. 28:19-20)?
2) How can we best serve people with a building (Matt. 20:28)?
3) How can we be good stewards so that the building is maximized seven days a week (Matt. 25:14ff)?

The answer: the nZone. The idea is as fresh as the morning sun, but the principles are as old as Scripture.

Even better, everyone who knows the story sees the divine fingerprints all over it.

- **Who owns the church: Am I driven by my desire for honor, or for God's honor?**

If God owns the church, I own nothing. Feelings of "holding" or "releasing" dissipate because I don't hold any of it in the first place. It's not unlike tithing. If you're a church planter, then you likely give your first ten percent in offering. How do you view the ninety percent you do not give? Stewardship 101 teaches that all we have is God's. The earth is the Lord's and everything in it. All cattle are His cattle. All cars are His cars. All fries are His fries. We may only give ten percent, but none of it is ever ours. So, even what I keep I do not hold. It is all His.

When I'm driven by my desire for praise, I look at the stuff in my hands (what I'm holding on to) and strategize how to invest it to advance my personal ambitions. But when I'm driven by my desire for God's honor, personal ambitions die. As the hymn "Rock of Ages," says, "Nothing in my hands I bring, simply to the cross I cling."

Who owns your church? Whose honor is really driving you?

- **Think Long-Term**

The other night I was the last to leave the office. The lights were out. The hall was dark. As I turned the key to set the deadbolt, a thought sobered me. *There will come a night when you turn this key for the last time. The next time this key unlocks this door, it will be held by another hand."* (A younger hand. Probably, a more athletic hand. I certainly hope a washed hand!—my mind strays easily.) That day, this office will welcome another leader. The chair will hold another who will write the next sermon and lead the next staff meeting."

With that, I turned away from the door and walked slowly to my car, reminded that it is not my church. It is God's church. Always has been. Always will be. Thank You, Lord!

Watershed Issue #2: The Essential, Irreplaceable Core Competency of the Church Leader
What is the most important quality of a church leader? Some would say vision. Without vision, well, you know... Important, but not it. Calling is up there, but not the primary one. Ownership of the church? Relates to the unchurched? Spousal support? All of these areas are huge, but not the essential, irreplaceable core competency.

Good news. Bad news. The good news is that this core competency is attainable for everyone. You don't have to be a superstar.

The bad news is that developing it is demanding and easily lost. The sad news is that no one champions this core competency much.

Before sharing the core competency, allow me to share my journey to this conclusion. As a church, we finally believed the time was right to build. We had some land, and we believed God had clarified the vision for how to build on the land. Specifically, we would build something that people who don't come to New Life would feel like is their building. The idea was that non-New Lifers would use the building so much to meet their felt needs that they would own the place. They would experience God's love before realizing it was God's love they were experiencing. That was the vision.

To build on that property demanded a $4 million capital campaign. Deep inside, I knew that was no problem. Secretly for years I had prayed a mountain-moving prayer that when the day arrived, we would get $6 million in our first capital campaign. So, we ran the campaign and knocked everyone's socks off with great vision and stories—and received just under $3 million in commitments. Ugh.

For months, we agonized. Do we downsize? How can we downsize without downsizing the dream? After all, the campaign was called, "More Than We Can See." If the campaign had been "Less Than We Can See," downsizing would have made perfect sense. How could we downsize and be faithful to the vision we believed God had led us to?

At this point, a developer in the church discovered an empty Anheuser Busch distribution center (which we affectionately labeled "The Bud Building"). The first time I walked into that building, I prayed impetuously, "God, if You give us this place, this would be more than we could have asked or imagined!" For two years, we negotiated with the owner. Eventually, we negotiated so long that the owner promised not to sell to anyone else without first giving us a chance to match the price. Finally, our elders believed we had done our best. We would sign the contract on Tuesday.

On Monday, we were informed that another buyer had signed. This was not a good day—far from it. This buyer was independently wealthy. As an owner of several patents, he would pay with cash—no need to be troubled with any bothersome financing issues. As the owner of several empty office buildings in northern Virginia, making the building immediately profitable wasn't a problem. Let it sit empty, take the tax write off, and sell it later after property values skyrocket, as they inevitably will. In short, we knew the Bud Building was gone. Fini. Kaput.

Thus began my season of second-guessing. At this point, we had worked on this dream of a community center-type building for nearly seven years. Each road had led to another dead end. Now, when we were on the verge of the dream taking flight, it dies. In that season, I asked the most important leadership question a church leader can ask, "Lord, do I still have the ability to discern Your leading?"

Through the years of leading New Life, I never felt like a ten talents-gifted guy, but at least I had a sense that I could discern God's next step for New Life and lead a key core of people to follow. But now I had to honestly ask myself, *Have I created this vision for New Life out of my own making? Has all this just been my idea that I have to try to sanctify using spiritually sounding language? Lord, is my time here done?*

No moment of clarity in ministry may ever surpass the moment when I realized, *If I cannot discern God's leading for this church, I am done. Nothing else matters.* By the way, the flip side is also true: Nothing matters more than having the ability to discern God's leading for the church and to help others obey. If you can do that, what else can matter more?

> *Trust in the Lord with all your heart,*
> *And lean not on your own understanding;*
> *In all your ways acknowledge Him,*
> *And He shall direct your paths* (Prov. 3:5,6).

Now, the rest of the story (I miss Paul Harvey). Three months passed. In that time, several indicators (mostly, the wisdom of our elders) led me to believe that God was leading us to move forward. We continued to look for another building that might be better suited for the vision. Nothing worked as well. Nothing was priced as well or had the same prime location.

September rolled around. The Bud Building owner called. "The buyer backed out."

I was stunned (though people in leadership with greater faith than I were not surprised). Three months earlier, we were ready to offer $7.1 million. The owner went on, "The buyer backed out. Are you still interested in buying the building?"

After a little back and forth, we signed a contract for $6.1 million. In three months, God saved us $1 million (even in Washington D.C., that's serious money!)

No human knows how to multiply the church in 50 years. But God does. And, when He does, the path He will choose will be unpredictable. We will plan, pray, work and sacrifice, but He will give life in places that look like death and will kill things that look like life to us. God's ways are higher than ours. Like seeds scattered indiscriminately by the sower, we won't always know which seeds will produce one hundred fold as we sow them. So, if your church and mine are to be part of a multiplication movement, the key is discerning God's leading every day, in hundreds of small ways, trusting that if we're faithful in little, He will produce more than we could see.

Watershed Issue #3: Is it better to have loved and lost than never to have loved at all?

Thomas Paine famously observed, "What we obtain too cheap, we esteem too lightly: it is dearness only that gives every thing its value. Heaven knows how to put a proper price upon its goods…" For church planters this means that if multiplication is more valuable than addition, the price will be high. Perhaps the greatest obstacle I need to overcome to lead from addition to multiplication is the price barrier.

I wish it were possible to count the number of times in ministry when—knocked down by a frustrating failure, untruthful criticism, or a surprising betrayal—I've wondered, *Is it really worth it?* Now, the problem may simply be that my jaw is pure glass. My wife insists that my pain threshold is low enough for an ant to step over it with ease. Still, I have listened to enough ministers to suspect I'm not alone.

Perhaps, seminary should include five years in the Marine Corps to toughen our mettle. Until then, we will only move from "addition" to "multiplication" once we settle the issue of price. What price are we willing to pay? What do you love that you're willing to sacrifice for multiplication? Is it better to risk and lose than never to risk at all? Is it better to love God and people and yet lose big, than never to have loved at all?

Romantics quickly jump in, "Yes!" "Go big, or go home! Nothing ventured, nothing gained! A pint's a pound the world around! (romantics aren't always the most logically coherent, you see).

The more circumspect hesitate. *Rolling Stone* magazine once polled its readers on the question, "Is there anything that would motivate you to die for your country?" Forty percent said "No." My hunch is that somewhere on their journey they had loved and lost, and discovered the losing is too painful. Forty percent said, "If it's just about my country, it is better not to lose."

If I'm honest with myself, that is where my heart leads me, as well. If you were around in 2003, you may not recognize the name Aron Ralston, but chances are you heard his story. Born on the glacial floodplains of Ohio, Ralston preferred hiking the mountains of Utah, but it cost him dearly. Caught under a boulder, Ralston survived by cutting off his own right forearm using a dull knife. Is it better to have loved and lost than never to have loved at all when you lose your right arm? Ralston's answer would differ from mine.

I posed the question to a room of church planters recently: "Is it better to have loved and lost than never to have loved at all?" To my left, a young church planter shook his head without hesitation. He had loved and lost more than his right arm. He loved and lost his marriage. Despite his sincere effort, she abandoned him. My friend's pensive nod said it all. In reality's grit and grind, there is little romantic about loving deeply and losing dearly.

How would you answer? Are you ready to pay the price for multiplication?

New Life Christian Church launched her first campus church plant in obedience to the challenge of Matthew 25. In most ways, our dreams for that plant never materialized. Initially, the risk created a momentum drag on all of our ministries. For a while, love for lost people produced more loss than gain. In private moments, we second-guessed. Glass jaw squarely struck, I would look up wondering, *Is it worth getting up? Trying again? What kind of idiot gets up knowing he'll just get punched again!* (Answer: this kind of idiot.)

So, be ready. A.W. Tozer once wrote that it's "doubtful whether God can bless a man greatly until He has hurt him deeply." To me, this may be the severest test of multiplication. Dare to attempt great things with God, be prepared to lose great things along the journey.

Habakkuk felt this test:

O Lord, how long shall I cry,
And You will not hear?
Even cry out to You, "Violence!"
And You will not save (Habakkuk 1:1).

Yet, the prophet persevered, and recalibrated:

Though the fig tree may not blossom,
Nor fruit be on the vines;
Though the labor of the olive may fail,
And the fields yield no food;
Though the flock may be cut off from the fold,
And there be no herd in the stalls—
Yet I will rejoice in the Lord,
I will joy in the God of my salvation.
The Lord God is my strength;
He will make my feet like deer's feet,

And He will make me walk on my high hills
(Habakkuk 3:17-19).

Every church planter aspiring to multiply would do well to embrace Habakkuk's vision. For most, the greatest obstacle to multiplication will not be strategy, ability, or resources. It is a test of will—the will to love and to lose and to continue to rejoice, confident that your labor is not in vain. He will make your feet walk on high hills.

If we would learn, God would teach us this truth didactically. Jesus taught that it is indeed better to love and lose in John 15:13: "Greater love has no one than this: that he would lay down His life for a friend." Of course, Jesus modeled this truth, as well, when He started the greatest multiplication movement in history with the greatest loss in eternity. Read Philippians 2:4-11 slowly.

Let each of you look out not only for his own interests, but also for the interests of others.
Let this mind be in you which was also in Christ Jesus, who, being in the form of God, did not consider it robbery to be equal with God, but made Himself of no reputation, taking the form of a bondservant, and coming in the likeness of men. And being found in appearance as a man, He humbled Himself and became obedient to the point of death, even the death of the cross. Therefore God also has highly exalted Him and given Him the name which is above every name, that at the name of Jesus every knee should bow, of those in heaven, and of those on earth, and of those under the earth, and that every tongue should confess that Jesus Christ is Lord, to the glory of God the Father.

In ways no theologian can comprehend, Jesus lost what it meant to be God in eternity to become God-man in time. Because of love, He lost. He lost Heaven. He made Himself nothing, a man of no reputation, not *despite* being

God, but *because* He is God. Why? For obedience to the Father—absolutely. And, for you. Jesus' way to you led through the way of the cross. This is Jesus' scheme of redemption. Strategically, it is God's sanctioned road to multiplication.

Unfortunately, I'm a slow learner. Wiser people learn from others. My mom always said that I was my own worst enemy because I always had to learn the hard way. For slow learners like me, God has a remedial school metaphorically located at the cliffs of Pointe du Hoc.

President Reagan was often called, "The Great Communicator." Speeches like the one he delivered overlooking Pointe du Hoc on the 40th anniversary of D-Day earned him that moniker. In front of Reagan that day sat aging U.S. Army Rangers; standing behind him, the monument to their honor. It was on this very spot forty years earlier that these men, who loved their country more than themselves, risked all to save a generation from tyranny. On D-Day, Pointe du Hoc was the primary target for the U.S troops—a one hundred-foot perpendicular wall defended by six 155mm German cannons. The men knew the insurmountable cliffs had to be taken, or the day would be lost.

Written by speechwriter Peggy Noonan, the heart of Reagan's tribute captures the transformational power of Pointe du Hoc: "These are the boys of Pointe du Hoc. These are the men who took the cliffs. These are the champions who helped free a continent. These are the heroes who helped end a war."

Boys. Men. Champions. Heroes.

Call it the way of the cross. Call it the cliffs of Pointe du Hoc. Call it what you will—every church planter must face it. Eventually, every church leader finds himself/herself at the base of an unscalable cliff where all must be risked for all to be won. Take the wall, and, not only will you discover no end to the ripple effect your risk will have on others, but also God will change you, as well. Boys. Men. Champions. Heroes.

As my Greek professor was so fond of saying, "God allows us to suffer today to prepare us for greater suffering tomorrow." (Somehow, I never found that as encouraging as he did!) In other words, because God's supreme strategy is the way of the cross, He teaches us this through others, or He will teach us at the base of Pointe du Hoc.

If you're like me, however, life is not math, where you master counting and therefore count with proficiency the rest of your days. For me, life is more like hitting a golf ball: I've never quite learned how to hit it well, and what I do learn I tend to forget before the next round.

So, may we listen. May we learn. This is not merely a church-planting multiplication strategy; this is the central truth of life. C.S. Lewis captures this powerfully in *Mere Christianity*.

"The principle runs through all life from top to bottom. Give up yourself, and you will find your real self. Lose your life and you will save it. Submit to death, death of your ambitions and favourite wishes every day and death of your whole body in the end: submit with every fibre of your being, and you will find eternal life. Keep back nothing. Nothing that you have not given away will ever be really yours. Nothing in you that has not died will ever be raised from the dead. Look for yourself, and you will find in the long run only hatred, loneliness, despair, rage, ruin, and decay. But look for Christ and you will find Him, and with Him everything else thrown in."

Want to start a multiplication movement? Don't focus on starting a multiplication movement. Love God, love lost people, and love the kingdom more than you love yourself and your vision and your church plant. Learn to love to lose. *Nothing that you have not given away will ever be really yours. Nothing in you that has not died will ever be raised from the dead.*

That is the way of the cross. That is God's strategy for multiplication.

Go Risk Something
Where do you go from here? Pray. Read the Bible. Seek wise, spiritual counsel. Seek the blessing of those in authority. Always begin there.

Now, go risk something.

Anne Lamott argues that the writer's worst enemy is perfectionism:

> *Perfectionism is the voice of the oppressor, the enemy of the people. It will keep you cramped and insane your whole life ... I think perfectionism is based on the obsessive belief that if you run carefully enough, hitting each stepping-stone just right, you won't have to die. The truth is that you will die anyway and that a lot of people who aren't even looking at their feet are going to do a whole lot better than you, and have a lot more fun while they're doing it."*

Every time I sit down to write a sermon, I think, *This is the week everyone discovers I have nothing to say. This is the moment I stand up in front of the congregation and they look at each other and ask, "What are we paying this moron?"* Great freedom is found in embracing that reality and risking to write a bad sermon anyway.

Your church will never discover her redemptive mettle until someone is willing to take a shot at multiplication—as ugly, imperfect, and open to valid criticism as your attempt will be! Try something. Take some next step—ugly and unstable as it may be!

Lamott continues:

Your day's work might turn out to have been a mess. So what? Vonnegut said, "When I write, I feel like an armless, legless man with a crayon in his mouth." So, go ahead and make big scrawls and mistakes. Use up lots of paper. Perfectionism is a mean, frozen form of idealism, while messes are the artist's true friend. What people somehow forgot to mention when we were children was that we need to make messes to find out who we are and why we're here—and, by extension, what we're supposed to be writing.

You will never discover who you are until you risk and lose. Your church will never discover the redemptive capacity God has placed within her until you're willing to fail and lose. And to try.

About the Author

Brett Andrews is the founding pastor of New Life Christian Church in the northern Virginia suburbs of Washington D.C. Since launching in 1993, New Life has grown to be a multisite church and has helped plant nearly 100 churches. The church also built a national church planting ministry, Passion 4 Planting, which has impacted countless other church plants by providing free resources and project management services.

In 1987, Brett met Laura, a season-ticket-holding Baltimore Orioles' fan, and knew it was love at first sight. Crediting Jesus and baseball for their wedded bliss, Brett and Laura recently celebrated 25 years of marriage with a trip to Major League Baseball's spring training camps. They are blessed with four children: three baseball players and a fast-pitch softball player.

EXPONENTIAL
RESOURCING CHURCH PLANTERS

- Largest annual gatherings of church planters in the world (Florida & Southern CA)
- 75+ FREE eBooks
- 400+ Hours of FREE Audio Training via podcasts from national leaders
- 30+ Hours of Video Training from national leaders
- FREE weekly email newsletter
- Missional and Discipleship Learning Communities
- Church Planters Blog
- Conference content available via Digital Access Pass

exponential.org >

@churchplanting
info@exponential.org

FREE EBOOKS

Igniting a Culture of Multiplication

Each author offers a transparent look at how their churches have embraced multiplication and have faced the inevitable tensions of creating a multiplication culture.

With 15+ National Leaders

Todd Wilson
Larry Walkemeyer
KP Yohannan
Brett Andrews
AJ Lall
Brian Bolt
Bob Roberts
Ralph Moore
Tim Hawks
Bruce Wesley
Steve Stroope
Oscar Muriu
Darrin Patrick
and more

WWW.EXPONENTIAL.ORG

EX
EXPONENTIAL CONFERENCE
April 27-30 | Tampa, FL
October 5-8 | Los Angeles. CA
SPARK
Launching and growing a Church is full of Tensions
We Shape our Culture out of our Tensions
At Exponential 2015 we will pursue together how to use our Tensions to shape a Culture of Multiplication
100+ Speakers | 9 Tracks | 5000 Church Planting Leaders
10+ Pre-Conference Forums & Labs | 20+ Bonus Sessions
exponential.org/2015east

KEEPING CHURCH PLANTERS
FOCUSED ON PEOPLE
PASSION FOR PLANTING OFFERS TOOLS AND RESOURCES DESIGNED TO KEEP TRACK OF THE DETAILS SO YOU DON'T HAVE TO. WHY? BECAUSE YOU WERE CALLED TO REACH PEOPLE. THE RESULT:
HEALTHIER CHURCH PLANTS AND HEALTHIER CHURCH PLANTERS.
OUR CURRENT OFFERINGS INCLUDE:
PlanterPrep
RESIDENCIES TO BEGIN YOUR PLANTING JOURNEY
PlanterApp
DISCOVER YOUR STRENGTHS
PlanterPlan
DEVELOP & MANAGE YOUR LAUNCH PLAN
PlanterAssist
TOOLS, FREE RESOURCES & MORE...
PASSION4 PLANTING
703.817.0601
PLANTING@CHURCH-PLANTING.NET
WWW.CHURCH-PLANTING.NET